Vanishings

Palewell Press

Vanishings

Poems – Rebecca Gethin

Vanishings
First edition 2020 from Palewell Press,
www.palewellpress.co.uk
Printed and bound in the UK
ISBN 978-1-911587-34-7

The cover design is Copyright © 2020 Camilla Reeve
The cover image of a Pine Marten and Red Squirrel is Copyright © 2020 Robert Adrian Hillman, downloaded from our image suppliers www.shutterstock.com
The interior illustrations are Copyright © 2020 Tom Harding
A CIP catalogue record for this title is available from the British Library.

Acknowledgements

With grateful thanks to the editors of these magazines / anthologies for including the following poems:

Holding the Night - Poetry Birmingham Review
Bog Creature - Butcher's Dog
Hypothesis - Crannog
Orison - The Lake
Extinct for 800 years, but… - Finished Creatures
Mover of Constellations, Maybe the Last Curlew on Dartmoor - Envoi
High Brown Fritillary - Emma Press' Insects anthology
Gannets - Palewell Press' *Welling Up*
Spirit Animal, Overlooked, Charm, Words for Wild
Choughs, Evening on Skomer, Secret life of Seals, Seven Sleeper - Foxglove
Fluke - Zoomorphic
Micromys Minuta, Backwater - Pennine Platform
Avocets - Atrium
Instar, Mots - recorded for Fiona Benson's Arts and Culture online anthology at University of Exeter.
Linnet, Peerie Deuk, Windfarers from *Messages* - published by Coast to Coast to Coast, 2019
Peerie-deuk commissioned by Beautiful Dragons' *Watch the Birdie*

Thanks

The following people and organisations helped me to meet all the creatures in this book so my grateful thanks go to all of the following:

John Walters who showed me the narrow-headed ant, the heath potter wasp, the horrid ground-weaving spider and told me about oil beetles; Jake Chant of Devon Wildlife Trust Beaver project who took me to see beavers and dams; Peter of Derek Gow Consultancy who showed me water voles, harvest mice and a beaver; Ardnamurchan Charters who would not turn for home till we had found White-tailed Eagles on Loch Sunart; Rothiemurchus Forest night-hide who let us stay out longer so we could see a pine marten; Nik Ward of BTO who let me handle a nightjar and who showed me the goldcrests; RSPB Devon and Matt Collis for showing me the waders; Cairngorm Reindeer Centre; Robin Hill who introduced me to dormice; Seaton Wetlands where I found a wild water vole; and Sarah at Devon Wildlife Trust's Harvest Mouse project. Thanks also to all my lovely friends in Litmus, especially Julie-ann Rowell and Bridget Thomasin; and the Company of Poets who have helped me edit many of these poems and to Gill McEvoy who gave the manuscript a good dose of spit and polish and Helen Evans who said all poetry books need a dipper poem.

Dedication

To Chris, my best-buddy and fellow
wildlife-watcher.

Whether we and our politicians know it or not, Nature is party to all our deals and decisions, and she has more votes, a longer memory, and a sterner sense of justice than we do.

There are moments when the heart is generous, and then it knows that for better or worse our lives are woven together here, one with one another and with the place and all the living things.

Wendell Berry: Essays

One touch of nature makes the whole world kin

Troilus and Cressida

Contents

Extinct for 800 years, but…

in the gathering of waters
among gaffling ducks
wind cockling
among sallows
sappy cresses and scorpion grass
we jabble and work it
moulding its flow
to our needs

we feel currents and eddies
in whiskers in skinwebs of feet
we must stopitup
dam it with sticks
saplings trees stalks
and with fixings and joints
we halt it pool it
hold it back

in the quiet of still water
we wrap ourselves
sink ourselves
in the dark of safekeeping
we keep it back
keep it in
keep it quiet keep it
still

/continued

culled from your language
no folk words survive
stripped of fur and scent glands
now you only catch
our tail-slap in names
of rivers and valleys
where still waters
are quiet

Mots

We needed to name
what we hadn't found words for...
wrote *burnished brass, blood-vein, lead belle.*
They came like missives from ourselves.

Their attraction to lights (mistaken for moon)
is what erased them
in their thousands
clouded magpie, lute string, hebrew character.

The smallest need a microscope
to tell them apart,
and can only be addressed in Latin
cryptoblabes bistriga, phycita robrella.

Now that they've been pinned
to illustrations
we'll only remember
the meanings of the old words

by the hieroglyphs on their wings
while they vanish, year
by year, word by
word – *engrailed, merveille du jour.*

Holding the Night

Its body is all feather and bone.
                                 I bring it close
wrapping my fingers over its wings.
                                     My fingertips answer
its bounding heart
               as if together they created vibrato.

It weighs almost nothing:
                       a ribcage enclosing
the inner life
             air between wing coverts
silks rubbing.

With one wrong squeeze
                     it might shatter into birds.
I could fall into the gaping beak
                       vanish in the pink gullet.
Eyes reflect glints of star.

The moon has thumbed
                  its name on wing and tail.
Flight is a living thing:
                  only by being so light
can it fly so far and carry the dark.

Instar

I stumble over islands of tussocks
among bogsquelch and gurgle

a clatter of stream nearby
tricklings from underboot.

But to see butterflies
I need butterfly vision,

switch focus from what's below
look further, across a small immensity

over reeds and willows
to spearwort, ragged robin

where flight conjures itself, rising
and dipping (or was it a flicker of light?)

and whatever it might be
I flounder towards, until there it is –

smaller than I remember, a gasp
in my throat. This phase is the briefest

the longest being the teem
of black larvae inside a spun web,

fattening on devil's bit scabious
when wings like light through stained glass

weren't even a dream.

Named for mud in Latin

With their heads deep in the cellars
of the estuary, bodies doubled
by reflections on the glisten,
inserting their bills to scrutinise
muddy water and watery mud
they must find more than worms
or molluscs, wrigglers in the salt flats –

whatever they find there
is mapped on their speckled feathering
in the white chevrons on outstretched wings
that flash in sunlight because
they're the mudgod's emissaries,
bearing its name
in all the languages they migrate through.

Avocets

Like dance notation writing itself
across the blank sheets of the muds
they run and walk, pause
and move on, swishing
their upturned beaks from side to side
through shallows and deeps,
each stilt-thin elegance
a twosome in counterpoint,
before the corps de ballet takes flight
from the stage of tides
forming their wing patterns
into a choreography of sky.

Orison

I keep searching, binoculars
to eyes, at the rosaries of kelp:
a priestly cormorant is alert on a rock.
Another dives and emerges
to distribute drips of blessing.

A blip of nose breaks slackwater
and my heart clutches
but it's a young seal rafting
who sinks back into
the nave of water.

On the shore it's all wetglitter
wrackfidget, the tide awakening
and gruntling at edges.
Slopflick of bladderwrack
skitters along edges of fronds.

(On my way I saw a spraint
and when I knelt to sniff
it smelt musky as incense.
It was here.
And a smeuse led from the beach.)

Every flitjink sets me on edge.
The harder I look
the less I see.
It might be wherever
I'm not looking

For me to ever see one
it mustn't catch my scent
the shine of my face
nor sense my shadow
as if my body were erased.

Backwater

Among reflections
    refractions of stalks
        stone-shine   waterwink   rain shirr

where tree-trunks wiggle
    shivery leaves blur
        their noses lead ripple trails

Along muddy edges   in squidge
    they gnaw out holeways   to guard
        with bicker and toothicuffs

where shadows that move spell danger
    they flop-plip   in a chorus
        of vanishing splishes

drippling   to weightlessness
    of sub-aqua   mudclouds
        they sink-in-a-blink

Beside or below   inside-out or back-to-front
    they burrow and frisker in what they embody
        water love   water soul.

Calibration of Loss

Beak-precise they prick insects and seeds
inhabiting flux and decay in carrs of willows
and alders, among bogrot and reeds.

In feathers of shadows and twig bark
willow tit calls are like small creaks of branches
about to break.

Bog creature

A toadlet monkeys through the trees
of reed blades and trunks of bulrush.

He acrobats between one that bends
and another athwart.

Once in a chorus of spawn
then a dizzy-swimming tadpole,

now his feet are tiny stars,
his jointed limbs have spring.

Every clump of reed is refuge,
quaking squish is hearth and home.

To escape my tread, he spirits
into the forest of moss and grass,

peeps out with wren-sharp eyes.
Less than a shiver in a tussock.

Micromys Minutus

I found a ball of grass among the hay. **John Clare**

Vertical tightrope artist
     in a swaying world
         she whisks
to the quivering seed head
      hardly bowing under
      mouse-weight.
Cheeks filled with grain
     she sprints head-first
         down the stem
     depending on
         thumbed hindfeet
     long claws and a tail
coiling to grip and balance
     among flux and risk
         to her nest-purse
     plaited between stalks
         and with no discernible door.

Horrid Ground-Weaving Spider

Their world is under a stone   or a piece of old carpet
      along a disused railway   a thread of trees
         between new housing and a road

They live in hollows   and creases
      hidden in money spider-size   two amber globules
         each one intricate as a gold tear

Sensing their way   feeling out sound
      with hairs on limbs   bristles on abdomen
         with blood-red palps

Weaving tiny maps   from their white spinnerets
      across nobbles   rough chinks
         in their underworld

When touched   say by a woodlouse   they run
      on segmented legs   clawed tarsi
         with precision instinct

Their brief existence   on the edge of Plymouth
      and known nowhere else
         in the universe.

Footnote: *the Latin name is Nothophantes horridus*

Syrinx

He keeps himself song-fit
so the muscles of his forked voice box
can reach his full range
of three hundred notes
The higher he flies
more and more song
soars through his bones
as the air sacs inflate
with the immensity
he scoops from sky and oxygen
giving it voice.

High Brown Fritillary

perhaps
  something
like … a match flame
or an electric impulse
darts
past your eye,
so you glance
      to focus
and   it's gone
       an inkling
you'd imagined,
      a bright flitting

one stops
on a bramble flower,
you spot its name
scribed on the wings,
opening, closing
feather-patterned
if you can decipher
quickly enough
the light and dark puzzle
of fritillary font

It happens again
beside
      beyond
           behind you
a chestnut flash
flick-darts just out
of your field
      of vision

leaving a patina
in air

A Charm

Red ants know beauty when they smell it
even before it crystallises into flight.
They bear the thyme-scented grub
looking and sounding just like one of their own
to their stronghold where guards salute
as they nestle it into the chamber.
Ten months they cradle it, all winter long,
overlooking how their charge chomps
through their own larvae. If questions are raised
it croons like their queen. Before it gets too fat
it unthreads its way through their labyrinth.
In sunlight its damp wings and antennae
open into a dazzle of blue.

Hypothesis

As if he laid secrets out in the cornfield
while calling all night

like a scraping of chainsaw teeth
you'll hear a kilometre away

so hesitant
he never flies away, keeping dead

still in the grass in the middle
of the field being mown

they say he lies on his back
holding the sky up with his long legs

he'd rather not be somewhere
but his voice won't stop repeating *crex*

crex and sky means so many distances
he might not be anywhere

Undertaking

Because she broke out
  of a sealed chamber
    she fashions clay amphorae

and punctuates the heath
  with a pottery of nests
    containing many meanings.

With a mouthful of water
  she kneads clay into a ball,
    flying to and fro all day in the sun

to mould each pot to a stem
  building it up layer by layer
    applying wet to dry.

It's a capsule/a calyx/a proxy womb
  for the egg she inserts inside
    and dangles by a thread

with a larder of paralysed caterpillars
  sealed in their tomb
    for the larva to feed on.

She checks her internal map
  looping round in a figure of eight
    over the lie of her ground –

stem and stone/ rock and scrape.
      Wind blows across the heath
          shaking the invisible urns.

If wasps metamorphosed
      in the heathers of your dreams
          you'd never find words for such intricacy.

Seven sleeper / thruddle-crump / hazel mouse

Under leaves, a furry apple of a one-ounce-mouse
sleeps fast in a cup woven with honeysuckle bark,
gaps darned with moss and grass blades.

It gorges on rosehips, hawthorn, blackberries
and hazel nuts, leaving nibbled holes in the shells.
Before seven months of sleep it must be fat.

With cold growing thicker, metabolism slows to tick-over
inside its core. The furred tail wraps the face
as it curls into the pips of its heartbeat.

Curiosity

A squall in the branches: a dash
of sunset with spine-splitting teeth
and grip-scoring claws.

A concertina of a creature
like incarnated ferocity
pours itself along pathways

of branches and trunk
out to dominions of scent
where nose is a state of being.

Nothing escapes needle-eyes,
ear-flick. Every hair of the coat
is primed to intuit forecasts

of threat and intention
With a pelage so deep and sweet
they've been skinned many times over.

Lek

This feather was a gift from a boreal forest:
tensive as though still attached
to the capercaillie's body.

Tail coverts once interlocked
quivering like a lady's fan,
the colour of pine forest humus

each one laced with a sprinkle of snow.
Imagining this pattern across the tail
I find myself in a woodland clearing

watching the lit-fuse of his display,
so absorbed he'd be an easy target.
His song of knife-sharpening

mesmerises me, though I know I should run
before he regains consciousness and targets me.
He's earned his epithet: *goat of the woods*.

Tears in the barbs are smoothed shut by my fingers
as if stroking could mend breaks
beyond hope of repair.

Cache

He knows every nobble and ridge
in the bark of each tree
every bend and crook of the branches
as if they were his own limbs.

As Yggdrasil's messenger and scout
he scurries from the top of the canopy
to the ground, connecting
the far-seeing of height with focus of depth –

in times of plenty he digs holes to squirrel
all messages out of sight.
When he forgets their whereabouts
these take root and grow into trees.

Antlers

They bear stillness like a crown
in the flourishes of branch and tine
covered in fur and pink with blood,
the shape a watermark or fingerprint.
If you so much as stroke it to feel the velvet
they swing their antlers at you
and stamp their feet. They speak to each other
with the click of their pastern joints
as they walk in each other's hoofprints
higher into the mountains.

Spirit Animal

A pale-coloured reindeer chooses you,
to link its fate with yours. It may take a death

from you. It circles round before laying itself down
in the snowfall of your dreams,

you know how far away it is by the waning of the moon.
In the dark you smell it, hear the grunting

and clicks of its feet as it rises
to leave you

with the bruises where someone has beaten it,
or with the crunch of lichen in your teeth.

Mover of Constellations

We looked for you from sky to sky
spotted the spread of angelic wings
over Camas na Gall, Ben Hiant.
    Shape-shifter, Wolfbane, Way-finder.

We imagined your far-seeing eyes
over mountains and sea, to islands
and headlands, under waters of loch and sea,
to low-tide reefs and glistening wrack.

We looked for you from ridge to summit
seized on three specks of you above
Oronsay, Camus nan Liath, Torr nan Con.
Too high and far for our eyes

only the spread of barn-door wings,
not feather tips lifting on updraft,
yellow weaponry. In other tongues
    Truth-finder, Bird of altars and prayer.

Footnote: Odin transformed himself into an eagle and was known by many names in Old Norse dialects and in various texts.

Adder

How I came to see it I don't know
as it didn't move, its head raised slightly
from the ground, poised as if about
to strike, its body looking soft
and strokeable – I almost did so –
while I stared at it and it at me
as though we were both caught
on the edge of our deaths.

Glints in the Echoes

an electrical pulse
in the air

a catch-dark
a draft on your cheek

just-glimpsed images
of winged night

a sound you barely
see on a frequency

too high to hear
a precision

instrument
as cochlea

catches each flutter
to glean moths

and winged beetles
among the density

of trees their wings
never touch a leaf

Once launched into sky there's no going back

Faith is the bird that feels the light when the dawn is still dark.
Rabindranath Tagore

There are times when you hear them
tearing over the rooftops and screaming
down alleyways. Aerial dolphins
with overlapping feathers tight as scales
and little hawk faces
the gape as wide as a slit throat
eyes as blue as gas flame.

Evenings, we'd sit on a bench together
watching the aerobatics
as screeching parties of youngsters
careered and wheeled
in the deep valley between mountains.
And I never gave it a thought –
that there'd be no going back.

Fluke

People wander the shore looking to sea as though waiting
for a god to manifest, or a sign of an epiphany, an oracle

from the expanse. We stare at the jostle of isosceles triangles
playing leapfrog over one another before they collapse

on the shingle, sibilant and fricative. Plenty of fish out there –
a gulp of cormorants sit poised on what can't keep shape,

outstretched wings a black witchery of fin. Gannets spiral,
strike it like lightning. After a pause they materialise, almost

gagging on their swallow, plunge upwards to free themselves
like shooting stars. All water is of a mind to rise, the force

of waves pushing from behind. A boom of a wave detonates,
spraying rainbows. Ground shudders. A snort like a horse.

Spouts of white spray as a shining hump back with a dorsal fin
arcs through the water, arc after arc, leaving roundels

of flat calm in its wake, printing stillness on higgledy water.
Its winged tail lifts before diving beyond our ken.

And that's when it seems the air is a hymn, the sea
a psalm in counterpoint.

Peerie-deuk

Small, querulous voices
among waves' quiver and heave
where they hide themselves

in shadow and light of their feathers.
As though only visiting this world
for insects and crustaceans,

they live on hinges of moments,
riding currents and tides.
Whirling on the surface of a lochan

like a *tottim* they create a vortex
to draw up creatures which they snap-peck
one by one, quick as chopsticks.

Males incubate eggs whose shells are dense
with legend as if each chick grew to fill its own map
inscribed by its mother. Females can't do

with running a nesthold, preferring to make
a head start on the 16,000-mile *vaege*
from Shetland to Galapagos.

Footnote:
Shetland dialect word for the Red-necked Phalarope is peerie-
deuk, a little clockwork duck.
A tottim is a spinning top.
A vaege is a journey by sea.

Omen

Head and beak snorkel it
through surf, body waltzing
through a lace of stirred spray.

It flips into spittlewater,
beakdiving through waves
and tunnelling down to the benthic.

It hears with all its body,
both prey and rocks belowater –
what visibility is there

in fizz and seethe? Each goingunder
is calibrated to how long
it can notbreathe.

It shoots out of the water
like a pip spat from lips,
like a single crotchet on a sheet,

where it conducts
the accelerando of waves,
as if it's the composer.

Secret Life of Seals

It starts with a breathhuff, a nosepush
a flippertouch
      a leantowards
          a snuggling
a bellyup, a heavingover
      a mutual slidealong
          sloping shingle into whoomf of bubble
in twirlsquirm
          and fangy tango lunge
             an almost do-si-do
a flippy tangle
      a wrap   a bit of tag   a lot of tug
          an ottering   a floating
among breakers
      a snorty swing out to the deep
          a break-neck-dash
between rocks and knotted currents
      diving into invisibility
          rising nose to nose   with oxter tingle
 with flipperslapping laughter
          waltzing with each other's tails
weightless   weightless

Gannets

On elbows of white wings
        dipped in jet
they ride along gulleys
of waves, rising
        over the crest
                as it topples,
beyond gravity –
aerial minesweepers
        with searchlight eyes.

On chimneys of updraft
they swirl round
        catch gusts on a slant
with tilted wings,
        flexing, tensing
        tightly reefed
knowing all the possibilities
        but easeful
as if they hunted
        with wind.

Spiralling higher
       they bullet themselves through water,
            vanishing   one by one
in a blowhole of spray,

     re-appear –

bottle on the surface   to swallow
shake out their wings
       for the up and aloft.

Choughs

call on one note
        to each another
                across the sky
from Kenidjack to Nanquidno,
        there and back,
                here again,
                        wing-fingers spread
        as they sidetumble from a height,
                swingrise on the curve
        of an updraft,
folding their wings,
        to freefall downcliff,
        chuffed to tool the gusts
                and perfect the precision
of their landing
        next to one another
                on a small shelf of rock.

Perhaps the last curlew on Dartmoor

Philosophers with half-moon beaks
used to discuss theories across the moors,
planting their starred feet on the squish
which they scrutinised
for wriggling clues, reflected in retinas.

But how quiet must we be
to hear the one bird calling,
the one no-one knows is there?
Its ululation across the marshes
could be wind through hollow reeds.

On wings the colour of sallows
and tussocks it drifts over glints
of peaty water and reed clumps
as though the mire's messenger
had taken to the air,

quartering the ground
looking for the connection
to make the world work better,
as he searches year after year
for a mate who never comes.

Natural Selection

By no standard of conduct, whether human or animal, can its habits of life be condoned. **Frances Pitt, The Scandalous Cuckoo.**

However long it takes, she lies in wait
to detect a pipit or a bunting flitting to and fro

their particular chirps and trills
imprinted in her bones through the air space

and membrane in the egg she broke out of
patterned to mimic the true ones in the nest -

that she'd learned from the dark-warmth
under the foster mother whose urge was to feed

the monster she'd hatched and had heaved
her own hatchlings out of the nest.

Later, taking no leave, cuckoos show fledglings
neither which way to go nor how far.

Windfarers

Winter alights with a squawk
in berried trees, or in a scuttling
across the land. Their skill is to ransack
clods and tussocks at a sprint.

The Anglo-Saxons named the bird
feldefar, traveller of the fields.
In Cornish, the word
is *shewollock*, the sly one:

Viking birds from across the North Sea,
helmeted in blue grey feathers
they run to a stop, stand erect,
take to the wind in a horde.

They watch from leafless trees where
like boats at anchor they all face
the same direction: snow-light
of their homeland under their wings.

The Goldcrest

dashflits along a bough, nips spiders and insects
among pine needles,
      its beak thin as a pin.

The weight of a larch cone it flies like a blink,
but flocks reach here
      from across the North Sea

sometimes resting on fishing boats. In summer
it is she who lines the nest,
      with cobweb, moss, lichen,

then sits tight on ten or more eggs
not once but twice,
      warming them

by inserting her thorntwig legs between.
The yellow-gold crest
      is a flitter of flame,

the voice a struck match, a flint-scrape
its frequency so high
      you barely catch

its syllable – but listen,
listen
      for the whirr of wings.

Spark

Hurrying water
breaks apart on boulders -
a flicker
like a struck match that almost ignites
         a crack in the light –
black river, flecks of white.

A dipper curtsies to the froth
churning in wavelets.
He opens his beak to sing
stares through the current snagging on his toes
steps down into the turbulence
disappears
steps out again
concentrates on flitgets
only he can see down there.

Linnet

A sprinkle of joy in the wind
and there it is
as if laughing took form
poised on the top twig of a gorse bush
a pink blush, chestnut flecks
a little fanfare of whistles
a glimpse of song
a turning in air,
a dart, a trickle of energy
holding on
letting go

A Summoning

If I guess your true name
will you come to me?

Is it …
Nose squiffler   Winter nester
Worm boggler   Needle creature
Thrupennybeast   Eggthief
Night haunter   Owlcritter
Beetle muncher   Sniffter
Slugsucker   Fleatrap
Spikey mouse   Thornyball
Sticklecoat   Hotchipaws
Moon-grunter   Hedge-fidge
Leafhogger   Groundurchin
Stinkanointer   Badgerbait
Fortuneteller   Friendmaker
Witchyspine   Yellowpins

One last try… Is it perhaps Bumplypricklepin?

Overlooked

Beside the A road, a scrubby place
of rough grass, bramble, gorse –
land to make a developer think
depot, warehouse, lorry park,

where each nest opens through a grassy tussock
you'd never notice
were it not for the little fringe of thatch
of fine grass blades, chewed into short lengths.

The focus is on the sun at its zenith
where they bring their rice-grain eggs
for warmth as they turn into larvae,
mandibles first, then eyes,

later the intestinal tract and limbs.
Pupae slough off the egg-skin
and as they waken into being an ant
they know exactly what to do

all of one mind, to be *formica exsecta*
or ant with notch in head.
Colonies spread under and over ground,
all individual notes in a score,

filling the staves of their territory.
They run between grasses and plants,
up low birches to farm their aphid flocks,
tending them, nuzzling them

to let down honeydew drop by drop,
filling the vessels of themselves
to transport this sweetness
back to the brood chamber.

In this one place, heathland
of no value except for what lies below
there's a world of difference
between *exsecta* and extinct.

Across the road and camouflaged
by a high hedge, a china clay pit
bays and growls,
bulldozers digging and scraping.

Why oil beetle larvae have three claws

The mining bee isn't aware
as she grazes on the field of a flowerhead
that *triungulins* have made it their lair.

They scramble into her gingery fur
while she's preoccupied with nectar and pollen.
Sticking to her body like tiny burrs

they ride piggyback to her nest in her burrow.
Here they feast on eggs and stores,
pupate for the winter and follow

the light at the end of the tunnel in spring
to lay thousands more eggs nearby
without any tell-tale *cuc-koo-ing*.

Lives being lived

I never knew they were there
until I scanned the oaks by torchlight
and spotted a glittery oval disc
hurrying over the ridges of bark
on armoured legs
scouring the territory
for the scent or feel of tree slugs –
another locked into a victim
to inject it with digestive juices
and extract the fluids
in a gradual emptying of skin
knowing something I didn't
about cells coming round
to discover themselves
inside another being
its metallic blue-purple elytra
rough as the moon's surface.

Twilight on Skomer

Above the cliffs a swarm
of sea birds circles
the cinched waist of the island
a carousel of puffins and auks
flying higher, faster,
almost silent except for beating wings
squawks from their audience
on ledges and in burrows –
a dervish dance
a typhoon rooted in one place
a lighthouse beam of dark motes
a spell to herald darkness
praise for another day of incubation
this ritual of summer evenings
and my small white face
watching from the bobbing boat.

Harescape

She kicks out a form for each of her leverets
pressing down stalks and blades to conceal them
in the hurlygush of wind through grassland.

Leaving them in the care of their hearing and acuity,
she returns only once a day to suckle them.
Safer without her, they must discover

the shapeshifts of daylight and dark for themselves
scrying among seedheads
the opening and closing of star flowers,

how to distinguish the pulse and smell of a feartide
which synapse conjures into pull of sinew,
jolt of paw pad on sward - their gift for vanishing.

Bestiary

Extinct for 800 years, but	Beaver
Mots	Moths recorded in Devon
Holding the Night	Nightjar
Instar	Marsh Fritillary
Named for mud in Latin	Black-tailed Godwit
Avocets	ibid
Orison	Otter
Backwater	Water Vole
Calibration of Loss	Willow Tit
Bog Creature	Common Toad
Micromys Minutus	Harvest Mouse
Horrid Ground-Weaving Spider	ibid
Syrinx	Sky Lark
High Brown Fritillary	ibid
A Charm	Large Blue Butterfly
Hypothesis	Corncrake
Undertaking	Heath Potter Wasp
Seven sleeper	Dormouse
Curiosity	Pine Marten
Lek	Capercaillie
Cache	Red Squirrel
Antlers	Reindeer
Spirit Animal	Reindeer
Mover of Constellations	White-tailed Eagle
Adder	ibid
Glints in the echoes	Greater Horseshoe Bat
Once launched into sky	Common Swift
Fluke	Hump-backed Whale
Peerie-deuk	Red-necked Phalarope
Omen	Shag
Secret Life of Seals	Atlantic Grey Seal
Choughs	ibid
Gannets	ibid
Perhaps the last curlew on Dartmoor	ibid

Rebecca Gethin - Biography

Rebecca Gethin lives on Dartmoor in Devon. Publications include *A Sprig of Rowan* (Three Drops Press 2017), *All the Time in the World* (Cinnamon Press 2017), *A Handful of Water (Cinnamon Press)* and two novels. In 2017 she edited an anthology of poems about elephants to help raise money for an elephant orphanage in Kenya.

Rebecca has been a Hawthornden Fellow and jointly won the 2018 Coast to Coast to Coast Pamphlet competition with *Messages*, a small, limited edition pamphlet. She was awarded a writing residency at Brisons Veor in Cornwall and Marble will publish a chapbook called *Fathom*.

Features include Ways with Words at Dartington, Words and Ears, Pembroke Poets in Oxford, Buzzwords in Cheltenham and she represented Coast to Coast to Coast at Aldeburgh Poetry Festival. She has also been a Poetry School tutor.

Rebecca will be donating her proceeds from sales of the book to a number of conservation charities.

Palewell Press

Palewell Press is an independent publisher handling poetry, fiction and non-fiction with a focus on books that foster Justice, Equality and Sustainability. The Editor can be reached on enquiries@palewellpress.co.uk